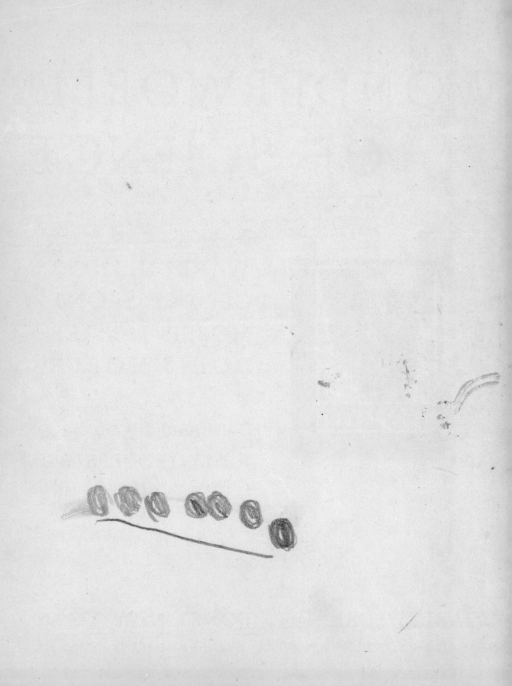

# THE
# WONDERWORLD
# OF SCIENCE

By

## WARREN KNOX
## GEORGE STONE
## MORRIS MEISTER
## DORIS NOBLE

•

Illustrated by
## ALMA FRODERSTROM

*Book Two*

## CHARLES SCRIBNER'S SONS · NEW YORK
### CHICAGO · BOSTON · ATLANTA · SAN FRANCISCO · DALLAS

# ACKNOWLEDGMENT

The authors wish to thank all those who have assisted in the development and trial of the materials used in this series. Experimentation was concerned particularly with pupil interest, grade placement, appropriateness of activities, and reading comprehension. The authors are especially grateful to the following teachers and supervisors who have been generous in their contributions to this textbook project:

MISS LOUISE ADAMS, Teacher in Primary Grades, School 16, Albany, N. Y.

MRS. FAITH LE FORT DUFFY, Teacher in Primary Grades, Edgemont School, Scarsdale, N. Y.

MISS CATHERINE DUTWEILER, Teacher in Primary Grades, East Street School, Hicksville, N. Y.

MISS NELLIE GRIFFITHS, In Charge of Elementary Work, Training School, North Texas State Teachers College, Denton, Texas.

DR. B. B. HARRIS, Dean, North Texas State Teachers College, Denton, Texas.

MISS MOLLY MAE HARRIS, Specialist in Reading, East School, Long Beach, N. Y.

MISS ELEANOR B. MASON, Librarian, Edgemont School, Scarsdale, N. Y.

MRS. HELEN MILLER, Teacher in Primary Grades, Nicholai Street School, Hicksville, N. Y.

MISS AGNES MONAHAN, Teacher in Primary Grades, School 16, Albany, N. Y.

MISS NINA PLANTZ, Principal, East Street School, Hicksville, N. Y.

MISS CARRIE M. SMITH, Cold Spring Harbor, N. Y.

MISS TAMAR WHEATER, Teacher in Primary Grades, Nicholai Street School, Hicksville, N. Y.

MISS EPSIE YOUNG, Teacher in Grade Two, Training School, North Texas State Teachers College, Denton, Texas.

Many thanks are due also to the hundreds of boys and girls who have served as willing and interested helpers during the period of trial and experimentation. The authors hope that children everywhere will be thrilled with their adventures in THE WONDERWORLD OF SCIENCE.

# CONTENTS

## ANIMALS AND THEIR FOOD

## GETTING READY FOR WINTER

## WATER AND ITS FORMS

# MAGNETS

# THE EARTH

# ANIMALS AND THEIR BABIES

# USEFUL AND HARMFUL ANIMALS

# ANIMALS AND THEIR FOOD

## Animals That Eat Plants

Many animals lived near the home of Jimmy and Alice.

Some of the animals were on the ground. Some were in the trees. Others were in the air or in the water. All of the animals were very busy.

"Why are the animals so busy?" asked
Jimmy one day. "I wonder what they
are doing."

"Let's watch them and find out," said
Alice.

First they watched the big animals in
the field. The animals were eating grass.
They ate and ate all day long.

Near the fields was a woods where wild
animals lived. Jimmy and Alice went
into the woods. They saw a deer. It was
so busy eating grass that it did not see
them.

"How pretty he is!" said Alice.

The deer looked up and then ran away
through the bushes.

"Now," said Jimmy, "let's watch some little animals."

In the field were many grasshoppers. They were eating grass leaves. When Jimmy and Alice came near, the grasshoppers jumped away and began to eat other leaves.

## Insects

The children went farther into the woods. Jimmy pulled some leaves from a tree.

"Look, Alice," he said. "Here are some little animals. They are eating these leaves. I think they must be insects."

"Yes, they are insects," said Alice, "because they have six legs. Father says animals that have six legs are insects."

Leaves are food for many kinds of animals. But animals eat other parts of plants, too.

The roots of plants make good food for some animals. Other animals like to eat buds and stems. Many kinds of animals eat fruits and seeds. Every part of a plant is food for some animal.

## Things to Do

1. Try to find some little animals on grass leaves.

2. Dig up a garden plant and look for animals that live on the roots.

3. Try to find a piece of wood that has been partly eaten by insects.

4. Look for some insects that live in water.

5. Grow some fruit flies in jars. Fruit flies like fruit to eat.

6. Look for insect eggs.

7. Find pictures of different kinds of insects. Put the pictures up in your room.

8. Look at plants near the school and find some of the animals that eat different parts of the plants. Try to find a big plant that has not been partly eaten by some animal. It will be hard to find.

## More Things to Do

Catch some insects in this way.

Look at an insect with a glass that makes it look bigger.

Count its legs.
Find its eyes.
Find its mouth.

Name the parts of this plant.
Which parts do insects eat?

## Playing a Game with Insects

Sometimes Jimmy and Alice play a game. They go to the garden where many insects come to visit the flowers. Jimmy and Alice each watch a flower. They watch the flower for a long time and count the insects that come to visit the flower. Sometimes more insects come to visit Jimmy's flower. Sometimes more come to visit Alice's flower.

Do you play this game? Jimmy and Alice think it is fun.

## How Insects Get Food from Flowers

Some kinds of flowers have a little sweet water in them. Insects like this water and come to the flowers to get it. Bees are insects that like to visit flowers.

An insect needs a long tongue to get the sweet water. It puts its tongue down into the flower. Then it draws up the water through its tongue.

Some insects roll up their tongues after they get the sweet water from flowers.

## Animals That Eat Animals

One day Jimmy and Alice were looking for animals near a lake. They saw a frog near the water. They watched the frog to see what he would do.

Then something very funny happened. A fly came near the frog's mouth. The frog put out his tongue very fast and caught the fly.

"I never saw a frog catch a fly before," said Alice. "How can he do it so fast?"

"A frog's tongue is very different from the tongues of most other animals," said Jimmy. "It is fastened to the front of his mouth. That is why he can put it out so fast."

"The frog's tongue went too fast for me to see how it was fastened," said Alice. "But now I know how he can get his food."

"Animals have to move fast to catch other animals," said Jimmy.

# Animals' Teeth

"Do very many animals eat other animals?" asked Alice.

"Yes," said Jimmy. "Some animals do not eat plants. You can find out what kind of food an animal eats by looking at its teeth. If it has long, sharp teeth, it eats other animals. Cats have long, sharp teeth. They eat other animals.

"If an animal has flat teeth, it eats grass. Cows have short, flat teeth. They eat grass. Horses and sheep have flat teeth, too."

"Some of my teeth are sharp and some are flat," said Alice. "What do I eat?"

"Some of your food comes from plants and some from animals," said Jimmy.

"Do all animals have teeth?" asked Alice.

"I do not know," said Jimmy.

## Some Things You Can Find Out

1. Do you know the answer to Alice's question?  How can you find out the answer?

2. Do you know how many teeth you have?  How can you find out?

3. What kinds of teeth do you have?  For what do you use each of the kinds of teeth that you have?

4. Does a bird have teeth?

## Things to Do

1. Look at a cat's teeth.  Tell how they are different from your teeth.

2. Look at a horse's teeth.

3. Find pictures of animals that have big teeth.

4. Find pictures of animals that have no teeth.

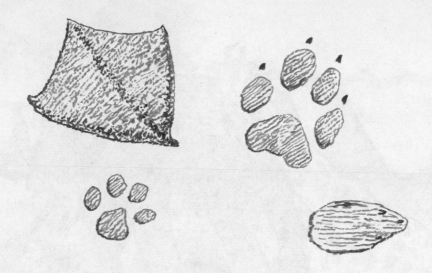

## Animal Tracks

It is fun to make foot pictures of animals. Put a stamp pad against the animal's foot. Then put the foot down on a piece of paper.

Here are some foot pictures that Jimmy and Alice made. They used a duck, a dog, a cat, and a rabbit to make the pictures.

Do you know which animal made each of the pictures?

## Animals at the Circus

One day Jimmy and Alice went to the circus. Here are some of the animals that they saw. Can you name them all? What other circus animals do you know?

It was fun to watch the circus animals eat. Can you tell which of the animals eat plants and which eat other animals?

It was fun to watch the circus animals drink. What animals have you seen drinking water?

# How Animals Get Their Food

Many animals keep very busy looking for food to eat.

Some animals have sharp eyes to help them find their food. Hawks, as they fly through the air, can see a mouse on the ground. When the hawk sees a mouse, he flies down to catch it. If the mouse sees him in time, the hawk does not have any dinner.

Some animals use their noses, and some use their ears to help them find food. A dog can smell the track of an animal. He keeps on the track and catches the animal.

Animals use their eyes, ears and noses to keep from being eaten. Deer and wild horses can smell other animals. Deer and horses use their eyes and ears, too. They run away when animals that might eat them are near.

Have you ever watched a cat trying to catch something to eat? A cat uses her eyes most in finding her food. A cat also uses her nose and her ears.

Look closely at a cat's foot. You will see the soft pads and the claws that she has. How do these claws help the cat to get her food?

When does a cat use her claws?

Some birds use their feet to catch animals.  Other birds use their bills to catch
their food.

Birds also use their wings and legs to
help them get their food.

"All animals have to eat something,"
said Jimmy to Alice one day.

"Many birds live on insects. Others
eat worms, and some eat fish. Bees get
their food from flowers. Grasshoppers
and cows eat grass. Frogs catch flies.
Ducks eat almost any kind of food. They
like plants, insects, fish, and frogs. But
I never saw a snake eat, did you?"

"No," said Alice, "but I know where
there is a snake. Let's watch him and
find out what he eats."

They found the snake by a big rock.
He was lying in the sun. They watched
and they watched and they watched. But
the snake did not try to eat anything.
He did not even move.

"Snakes do not seem to eat very often,"
said Alice.

Just then the snake jumped.

"Oooh!" said Alice, and she jumped, too.

"Look," said Jimmy. "The snake has caught a frog."

Soon the frog was inside the snake. He made a funny-looking lump in the snake's body.

"Let's go home," said Alice. "I don't like to see snakes eat."

"But the frog eats animals, too," said Jimmy.

"I know a good game we can play," said Jimmy, as they were going home. "Snakes eat frogs, frogs eat insects, insects eat plants. Now you tell me something that eats something that eats something else."

"Oh, I know one. Cats eat birds, birds eat worms, worms eat plants," said Alice.

"I know another one," said Jimmy. "We eat fish, fish eat mosquitoes, mosquitoes eat us."

"That was a funny one," said Alice. "I like this game. Let's play it some more."

# How Animals Are Protected

"I would not want any animal to eat me," said Alice. "Do all animals get eaten by other animals?"

"Many do," said Jimmy, "but other animals have ways to protect themselves.

"The frog was green like the grass. He was hard to see. He had big eyes that could see all around him. He had big legs and could jump very well."

"Yes," said Alice, "but the frog got caught."

"Sometimes frogs stay under water for a long time, where snakes cannot catch them," said Jimmy. "They can hide under rocks in the water.

"Large birds also like to eat frogs. Frogs jump into the water when they see a big bird coming. Birds often catch frogs if they do not jump soon enough."

# What Are the Right Answers?

1. An animal that has flat teeth is the
   bird          cow          cat
2. An animal that has no teeth is the
   bird          cow          cat
3. An animal that has sharp teeth is the
   bird          cow          cat
4. Butterflies get their food from
   flowers       leaves       animals
5. Grasshoppers get their food from
   birds         leaves       cows
6. Frogs get their food from
   flowers       leaves       animals
7. Horses eat
   insects       grass        birds
8. Animals with flat teeth eat
   birds         plants       insects
9. An animal that has six legs is the
   bird          cow          grasshopper

# Do You Know?

1. Name all the animals you know that eat plants only.

2. Name all the animals you know that eat animals only.

3. Name some animals that eat both plants and animals.

4. What kinds of food do birds eat?

5. What are some big animals that eat little animals?

6. What are some little animals that eat big animals?

7. What are some big animals that eat animal food?

8. What are some insects that eat other insects?

9. How do different animals catch their food?

10. In what ways are animals protected?

The animals in this picture are protected by their color. Can you tell how their colors make it hard for their enemies to find them?

The animals in this picture are protected in different ways. Can you tell
how each one is protected from its enemies?

# Do You Know?

Many animals eat plants.  What parts of plants do these animals eat?
1. Birds
2. Grasshoppers
3. Butterflies
4. Fruit flies
5. Cows
6. Rabbits
7. Horses

Every part of a plant is food for some animal.  Can you name some animals that eat these parts?
1. Leaves
2. Bark
3. Stems
4. Fruit
5. Roots
6. Flowers

# GETTING READY FOR WINTER

## Signs of Winter

It was cold one morning when Jimmy and Alice went out to play. Dark clouds were in the sky.

The wind blew through the trees, and the leaves came falling down.

"I have on my warm coat," said Alice.

"So have I," said Jimmy. "It feels like winter."

As the children played, they saw more
signs that winter was coming.  Many of
the flowers had gone.  The grass was
brown.

They could see only one animal.  He
was very busy looking for nuts.

"I guess he knows winter is coming,"
said Jimmy.

# Insects in Winter

"Where do all the insects go in winter?" asked Alice.

"Most of them die," said Jimmy. "Some of them hide in warm places. Some dig down into the ground. Others are busy all summer so that they will have food to eat in winter."

"I know that bees store up food for winter," said Alice. "But what do all the other insects eat in winter?"

"Many of them do not eat in winter," said Jimmy.

"Many insects lay eggs in the fall, and then die. They do not store up food as bees do.

"Other insects make cocoons. They live in the cocoons all winter without eating anything. Let us look for some cocoons. It will be fun."

Here are some cocoons that Jimmy and
Alice found. The pictures show what insects will come from them.

## Birds in Winter

Jimmy and Alice were looking for other signs of winter. They heard a noise in the air and looked up. "Oh, look at the birds!" cried Alice.

"I never saw so many birds," said Jimmy. "There are so many that I can not count them."

"What kind of birds are they?" asked Alice.

"They look like blackbirds," said Jimmy. "The blackbirds are going south. They seem to know that winter is coming."

"Why do birds go south in winter?" asked Alice.

"I think they go to get food," said Jimmy. "In the North there are no insects to eat."

"I know some birds that do not go south in winter," said Alice. "They find seeds to eat when the insects are gone. But they always look so cold. If I were a bird, I think it would be fun to go south."

"I think I would stay in the North," said Jimmy. "I would not like to fly so far. In the South there would be no snow to play in."

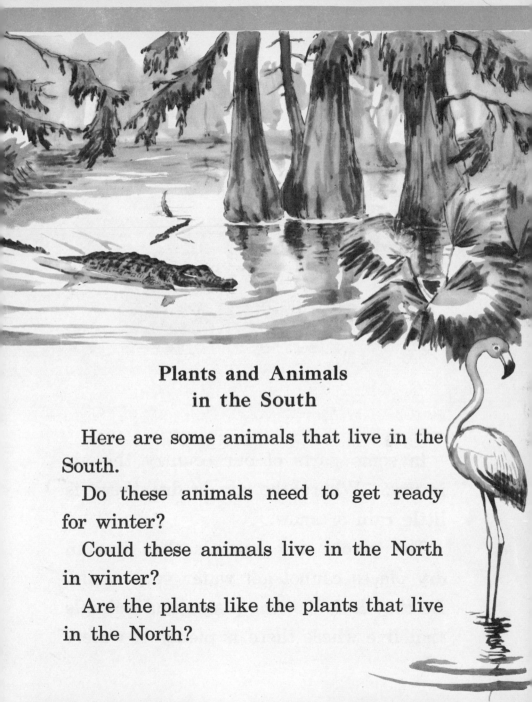

## Plants and Animals
## in the South

Here are some animals that live in the South.

Do these animals need to get ready for winter?

Could these animals live in the North in winter?

Are the plants like the plants that live in the North?

In some parts of our country the air
is dry. Where the air is dry there is
little rain or snow.

The plants and animals that live in
dry places cannot get water very easily.
Do they look like the plants and animals
that live where there is plenty of water?

## The Woodchuck

Jimmy and Alice were walking near the woods. They saw a hole in the ground.

"What is that?" asked Alice.

"That is where a woodchuck lives," Jimmy told her. "Let us see if he is at home. Put your ear to the ground and listen. I will make a noise with two rocks."

"I hear him! I hear him!" cried Alice. "He is at home."

"Then the woodchuck is not asleep yet," said Jimmy, "but he will be soon, I think. Woodchucks cannot go south as the birds do.

"In the fall they store up fat in their bodies. When winter comes, woodchucks cannot find any food. They dig holes in the ground and go to sleep. The fat in their bodies keeps them warm."

Here are some other animals that sleep
all winter.

They lie very still and breathe slowly.
They need very little food when they are
asleep.

## How Animals Get Ready
## for Winter

Many animals store food to eat in winter.

Some birds bring food to their nests. Ants take food into their homes. Bees make honey to eat in winter.

Sometimes rats and mice live in our houses. They take food and hide it.

Beavers cut down trees with their teeth.
Then they cut the trees into pieces and
store them away under the water. In
winter they eat the bark for their food.

The beaver in this picture is building a
house in the water.  The door of his house
is under the water.

The fox is an animal that does not get ready for winter. Foxes do not store food. They do not go to sleep. They do not go south. They can find food in winter. They catch mice, chickens, rabbits, and birds.

Frogs get ready for winter in a funny way. In the fall they dig holes in the mud. They go down into these holes and stay all winter. In the spring they dig their way out of the mud again.

People store up food for winter.

Here is one place where foods are stored.

Do you know another place where foods

are stored?

## Keeping Warm and Keeping Cool

It is easy for people to keep warm or cool. It is not easy for animals.

When the air is cool, we wear clothes that keep us warm. When the air is warm, we wear clothes that help us to keep cool.

In winter we heat the air in our homes. We heat the air in school. We make the air as warm as it is in summer.

When the air is warm in the house, we should not wear too many clothes.

| DAY | SKY | WIND | CLOUDS |
|---|---|---|---|
| Monday | | | |
| Tuesday | | | |
| Wednesday | | | |
| Thursday | | | |
| Friday | | | |

Alice watched the sky, the wind and the clouds every day. She made a picture of what she saw.

Can you tell the story of the days in Alice's picture?

Do you think Alice wore the same clothes each day?

We can change our clothes when it is too warm or too cold. Animals cannot do this. They protect themselves in other ways.

Sheep stand close together when it is very cold. Chickens go into their houses when it rains. Cows like to stay in the shade on hot days.

# Questions

1. Why do birds go south in winter?

2. How do animals keep warm in winter?

3. What do chickens do when it rains?

4. Name an animal that sleeps all winter long.

5. How can we make the air warm in winter?

6. What happens to insects in the winter?

7. What animals make cocoons?

8. Name some animals that store up food for winter.

9. Do people store up food for winter? Why?

10. Why should we take off our heavy clothes in a warm room?

11. What do sheep do on cold days? Why?

# Yes—No

1. All animals store up food to eat in winter.

2. Insects are animals.

3. Sheep go south in winter.

4. Woodchucks sleep in winter.

5. We should take off some of our warm clothes when we come into the house.

6. Bees store up food for winter.

7. All birds go south in winter.

8. Rats and mice store up food sometimes.

9. In some parts of our country it is very dry.

10. Many insects die when winter comes.

11. Woodchucks spin cocoons.

12. Birds have six legs.

13. Frogs fly south when winter comes.

14. Some animals sleep all winter.

# WATER AND ITS FORMS

## Things That Change

There are many stories of things that change. In one story horses were changed into mice, and mice were changed into horses. In another story a boy was changed into a frog.

Do you know any of these stories? Do you think they are true?

Does anything ever change into something else?

Here are some real changes that go on in the world.

How many things that change can you find in the picture?

When something changes, there is a reason for the change.

# Changes in Water

Water can change into ice. When water changes into ice, we say that the water changes its form. Ice can change into water. When ice changes into water, the form of water changes again.

How many forms of water do you see in this picture?

Are there any other forms of water?

# Things to Do

Here are some things you can do to find out more about the forms of water.

1. Heat some water and watch it change into steam.

2. Hold a cold piece of glass over the steam. Watch water form on the glass.

3. Put some water outside the window on a cold day and watch it freeze.

4. Put some salt with ice in a glass. What happens on the outside of the glass?

5. Put a little water into a small glass and set it in the glass with the salt and ice. What happens?

6. Watch snow and ice change into water.

7. Blow your breath on a cold window. Make a mark on the glass.

8. Heat a piece of ice until it changes into water and then into steam.

# Did You Find Out?

1. What makes water change into ice?
2. What makes ice change into water?
3. What makes water change into steam?
4. Can steam be changed into water?
5. Can steam be changed into ice? How?
6. Can water be changed into snow?
7. Can you see steam?
8. What happens to steam when it is cooled?
9. Can you see through water?
10. Does water have any color?
11. Is there water in your breath?
12. Is water that comes from ice the same as other water?
13. Can you name six different forms of water?
14. What forms of water do we get when water is cooled?

## Is Water Alive?

One day Alice said to Jimmy, "I think it would be fun to be a drop of water. Water moves around. Some of it goes into the clouds. The clouds move in the sky. Rain and snow fall from the clouds. Water from rain and snow runs into streams.

"Water never seems to stop moving. I wonder if water is alive."

"No," said Jimmy, "I do not think water is alive. Things that are alive can move without help. Water needs something to help it move. That is why I think water is not alive.

"There are many things I should like to know about water," he said. "I should like to know:

"How water gets into the clouds.

"What makes the water fall out of the clouds.

"What makes the clouds move.

"What holds the clouds in the sky.

"Where the water goes after it rains.

"Where the water goes when snow melts.

"What makes the waves.

"How many of these do you know?"

"I think I know one of them," said Alice. "I know what makes the waves."

## The Wind and the Waves

Alice put some water in a pan.

"Look," she said, "I can make waves when I blow on the water. When the wind blows on the water in the lake, the wind makes waves, too. But the wind can blow harder than I can. That is why the waves in the lake are so much bigger than mine."

"I think you are right," said Jimmy, "because when there is no wind there are no waves."

# Water in the Air

One day at school there was a pan of water on the table.

When Jimmy looked at it the next day, he said, "I think some of the water went out of the pan.  It is not as full as it was."

"Maybe the pan has a hole in it," said Alice.

The children looked.  There was no hole in the pan.

"Did some one take some of the water out of the pan?" asked one of the other girls.

No one had taken any of the water out of the pan.

"I guess a fly drank it," said one of the boys.  Then everybody laughed.

"Let us look at the pan tomorrow," said Jimmy.  "Then we will know if any more water goes out of the pan."

When the children looked in the pan the next day, the water was nearly gone.

"Where did it go?" asked Jimmy.

Can you answer Jimmy's question? Here are some things you can do to find the answer.

1. Fill a glass with water and set it on the window sill. See how long it will take for all of the water to go out of the glass.

2. Put some water in another glass. Put a cover over the glass. Watch to see whether any water stays in this glass.

3. Wash the blackboard and watch the water go away.

4. Set a big glass jar over a glass with water in it. Look at it the next day.

5. Put your hands in water and then hold them in the air. Watch to see whether water stays on your hands.

"How can we find out what makes water go into the air?" asked Alice.

"It might be heat," said Jimmy. "I know that it takes heat to make water change to steam."

Alice said, "I know what we can do. Let's put some water in different jars. Then we can put one in a cold place, one in a warm place, and one in a hot place. We can watch the jars and tell whether heat makes water go into the air."

Can you tell what the children learned?

When water goes into the air, it is called water vapor. There is some water vapor in the air all the time but we can not see it.

Water vapor gets into the air in many ways. Some of it comes from lakes and ponds. Some of it goes into the air from our bodies. Some of it goes into the air when clothes dry. How else does water vapor get into the air?

Sometimes so much water vapor goes into the air that little drops of water are formed. The drops are so small that they stay up in the air. They make a cloud. Then the little drops of water run together to form big drops. The big drops fall down as rain.

When a little rain falls, the water goes into the ground. If much rain falls, the water runs away on the ground.

Most of the rain water finds its way into streams. Little streams run into big streams. Big streams run into rivers. Rivers carry the water into the ocean.

The picture on this page shows a big waterfall. At some time all of this water fell as rain. It is on its way to the ocean.

## Water and Living Things

Most of our earth is covered with water. There is more water than there is land.

Many plants and animals live in the big oceans. There are more water animals than land animals. There are more water plants than land plants.

Here are some animals that live in the ocean. They swim in water. They find their food in water. They never come on land. How many of the water animals do you know?

The animals that live on land need water. In the far north it is so cold that the water is in the form of ice and snow. How do you think animals in the far North get the water they need?

Toads have a funny way of drinking water. They do not drink as other animals do. When a toad gets thirsty, he jumps into a puddle and drinks through his skin.

Did you ever watch a bird drink water?

How do other animals drink? Try to find out.

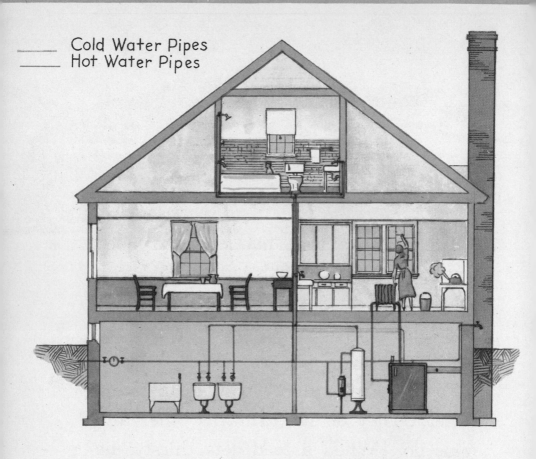

Cold Water Pipes
Hot Water Pipes

People cannot do without water. This picture shows some of the ways in which we use water in our homes. What uses of water are shown in the picture?

Can you name some uses of water that are not shown in the picture?

# Questions

1. What are some of the forms of water?
2. When does ice change its form?
3. What makes water change into ice?
4. Can water move?
5. Is water alive?
6. What makes waves?
7. What are clouds?
8. How do you know that rain comes from clouds?
9. How does water get into the air?
10. Can you see water vapor?
11. Where does the water go when you wash the blackboard?
12. What are some animals that live in water?
13. How does a toad drink?
14. What is water vapor?
15. What is the ocean?
16. How does water get into the ocean?

# Tell the Right Answers

1. When water is heated it changes into

    ice        steam        snow        iron

2. Waves are caused by

    fish        snakes        steam        wind

3. The thing that makes water go into the air is

    heat        cold        ice        toads

4. When steam is cooled it changes into

    heat        wind        waves        water

5. One form of water is

    heat        wind        ice        glass

6. A form of water that we cannot see is

    ice        vapor        snow        wind

7. Rain comes from the

    wind        clouds        sun        moon

8. Toads drink water through their

    mouth        feet        ears        skin

9. Birds drink water through their

    nose        ears        mouth        skin

# MAGNETS

## How Ships Find Their Way

The people who lived long ago were afraid of the ocean. They were afraid to sail ships far from land. Ships sometimes got lost when they were far out in the ocean.

The people wondered what happened to
the ships that got lost. They made up
stories about big animals in the ocean.
They said these animals ate the ships.

After many years people learned how to make a compass. The needle in a compass is a little magnet. A compass needle points north and south.

When sailors used a compass, they could find their way across the ocean. The compass always showed them which way was north. When people knew where north was, they could find south, east and west and could tell how to go home. The ships could find their way back to land. The people no longer told the stories about the big animals.

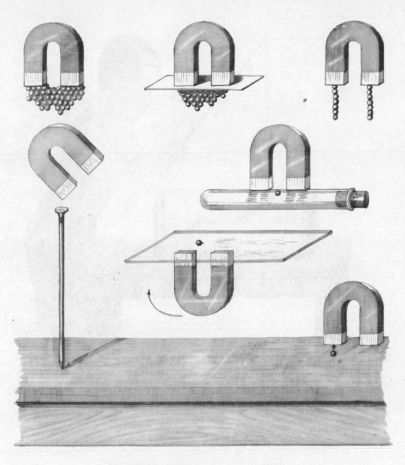

## What Magnets Do

Magnets pull things that are made of iron. It is fun to play with magnets. Here are some things you can do.

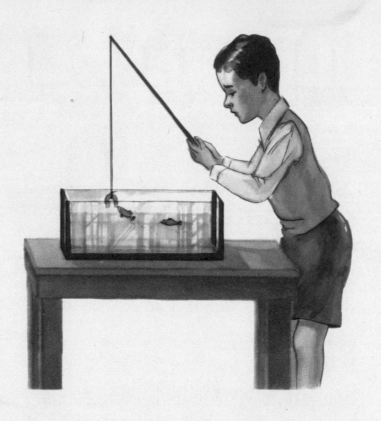

## Magnet Games

Some games are played with magnets. One game is fish pond. Each fish has a little piece of iron in it. You catch the fish with a magnet fish pole.

Some magnets are much stronger than others. Here is a way to tell which of two magnets is the stronger.

Tie a string around each magnet. Have both magnets touch a round piece of iron. Now pull on the strings. The stronger magnet will pull the piece of iron away from the other magnet.

Try this with different magnets.

## More Things to Find Out

Will magnets work through paper?
Will magnets work through wood?
Will magnets work through glass?

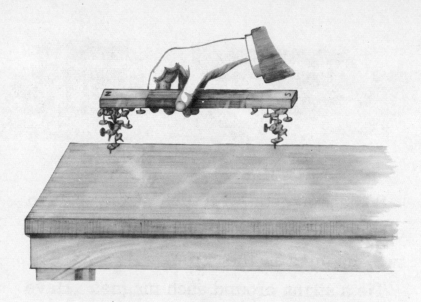

What parts of a magnet have the most
pull? Here is a way you can find out.

Place some little pieces of iron on the
table. Place a magnet on top of them.
Now lift the magnet.

Place some things that are not made of
iron on the table. Try to pick them up
with a magnet.

How can you use a magnet to find out
whether something is made of iron?

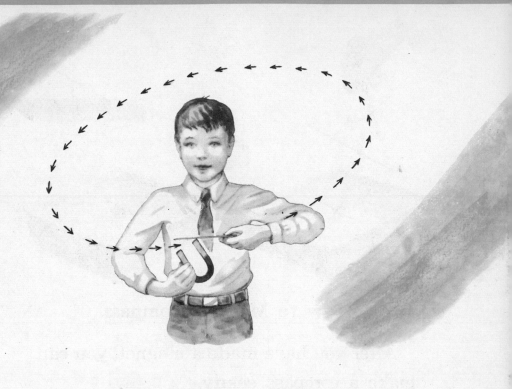

## How to Make a Magnet

It is easy to make a magnet. Here is one way to do it.

Rub a piece of steel across a magnet. Rub it across many times. Always rub it in the same direction.

Try your new magnet and see whether it works. Will it pick up pieces of iron?

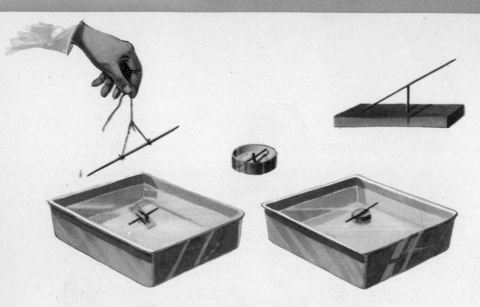

## How to Make a Compass

After you have made a magnet, you can make a compass easily.

Make a magnet out of a long needle. Hold up the needle in one of the ways shown in the picture.

Try your compass to see whether it works. Does the needle point north and south? Get another compass and see whether your compass points in the same direction.

## Things to Do

1. Bring a piece of iron near a compass. What happens?

2. Hold a piece of wood near a compass. Does anything happen?  Why?

3. Bring a magnet near a compass. What happens?

4. Try some other things to see whether they turn the compass needle.

5. Use a compass to find out whether something is made of iron.

6. Tell how you would use a compass to find south.

7. Tell how you would use a compass to find east.

8. Tell how you would use a compass to find west.

9. Tell how you would use a compass to find your way if you were lost in the woods.

## Do You Know?

1. What will a magnet do?

2. What will a compass do?

3. What games can you play with magnets?

4. How can you make a magnet?

5. How can you make a compass?

## Yes—No

1. A magnet will work through paper.

2. A magnet will pick up a piece of wood.

3. The needle of a compass points east and west.

4. Long ago big animals lived in the ocean and ate ships.

5. A magnet will pick up a piece of paper.

6. A magnet will work through glass.

7. The needle of a compass is made of wood.

# THE EARTH

## Meeting the Boat

One day Jimmy and Alice went to meet their grandfather. Grandfather had been away on a long trip. His trip had taken him around the world. Now he was coming home on a big ship.

Jimmy and Alice went to the dock with their mother. They were at the dock long before the ship came in. There were many other ships at the dock. It was fun to watch the ships coming and going.

At last they saw the top of a ship far
out on the ocean. After a long time they
could see more of the ship. The ship
seemed to rise higher and higher out of
the water.

## The Earth Is Round

"There must be a big hill in the ocean," said Alice. "The ship seems to be coming over a hill."

"Do you remember the picture of the earth we saw yesterday?" asked her mother.

"Oh, yes," said Alice, "I remember. The earth is round like a ball. It is not flat. That is why the ship seems to be coming over a hill."

When the ship came in, Grandfather
was on it.  He was very glad to see Jimmy
and Alice.  They asked him all kinds of
questions.  Jimmy asked questions about
the ship.  Alice asked questions about
the ocean and about the people who live
far away.

# The Pull of the Earth

There was a big globe in Jimmy's room. The globe was like the earth. The blue places on the globe were oceans. The other parts of the globe were land.

Alice said to Jimmy, "May I put my dolls on your globe? I think it would be fun to see where they came from."

"That will be fun," said Jimmy. "We will put some tape on their feet to hold them."

Grandfather told them where to put the dolls.

"Is that the way they should look?" asked Alice. "Some of the dolls are upside down. If the dolls were real people they would fall off the earth."

"But all of the dolls have their feet on the ground," said Jimmy. "People all over the earth walk with their feet on the ground. We always walk with our feet on the ground, don't we?"

"Then something must push us against the earth," said Alice.

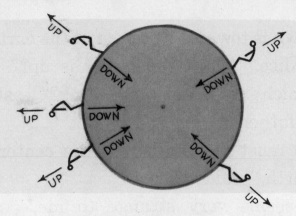

"No, nothing pushes us against the earth," said Grandfather. "It is the earth that pulls us. The earth pulls everything toward it. The pull of the earth is called gravity."

"Is that why things fall to the ground when we drop them?" asked Alice.

"Yes," said Grandfather, "gravity pulls them down."

"But which way is down?" asked Alice.

"I will draw you a picture," said Grandfather. "In this picture all of the people are pointing down."

"Down is toward the center of the earth," said Alice. "But which way is up?"

"Which way do you think?" asked Grandfather.

"Up must be away from the center of the earth," said Alice.

"It seems very strange to me," said Jimmy, "but I think you are right."

## Things to Do

Lift something. Can you feel the pull of gravity?

Lift one book. Now lift six books. Why are six books heavier than one?

Weigh yourself to find out how much the earth pulls on you.

Tie a rock on a string. Tie the other end of the string to a stick. Hold up the stick and move the rock away from you. Why does it move back?

## What Holds Up the Earth?

Long ago some people thought that a big elephant held up the earth. They thought that a big turtle held up the elephant.

Could an elephant hold up the earth? What would hold up the turtle?

There were other people who had a different idea. They thought that the earth floated in an ocean so big that no ship could go to the end of it.

Alice made a picture of the earth. Then she put clouds, birds and airplanes in the air around the earth. All around the earth is a thick covering of air. Above the air there is empty space.

The earth is like a big ball. It moves in empty space.

The sun and moon also move in empty space. They are big and round like the earth.

# Questions

1. What pulls a ball down when you throw it into the air?

2. Why does water run down hill?

3. Why does it take so long to go around the earth?

4. What pulls you back to the earth when you jump?

5. How do we know that the earth is round?

6. How do we know that the earth is big?

7. What is all around the earth?

8. What would happen if there were no gravity?

9. Which way is up?

10. Which way is down?

11. Why do some things weigh more than others?

12. Why will a ball roll down hill?

## Tell Why

1. We do not fall off the earth.
2. When you throw a ball into the air it comes down again.
3. Water runs down hill.
4. It takes a long time to go around the earth.
5. There seems to be a hill in the ocean.
6. Things never fall up.
7. Some things are heavier than others.
8. Air does not leave the earth.

## Tell Why Not

1. An elephant holds up the earth.
2. We can see across the ocean.
3. People on the other side of the earth stand on their heads.
4. We can walk across the ocean.
5. The earth is flat.
6. Cows can jump over the moon.

# ANIMALS AND THEIR BABIES

## Animals on the Farm

At Easter Jimmy and Alice went to see their cousins. Their cousins were Tom and Betty. They lived on a farm.

There were many animals on the farm. Some of them were baby animals. Tom took Jimmy to see some of the animals. Betty took Alice to see others.

The animals that Alice wanted to see
first were the chickens.

The baby chickens were very little.
Alice picked them up and petted them.
The mother chicken did not like that.
She was afraid that Alice would hurt her
babies.

Tom and Betty took Jimmy and Alice to see the other animals. They learned that baby animals are always hungry.

All the farm animals care for their babies in some way. Some animal mothers give milk. Milk makes the babies grow. When the babies grow bigger they eat other food.

Some animal mothers do not give milk. But they protect their young and find food for them.

Jimmy wanted to see the baby rabbits. At first Tom could not find them. The mother rabbit had covered the baby rabbits with dried grass.

"Why did the mother rabbit hide her babies?" asked Jimmy.

"She does not want us to look at them," said Tom. "She is afraid we will hurt them. There is another reason, too. Baby rabbits do not have much hair. The mother covers them up so that they will be warm."

Tom told a story about his pet hen. The hen laid an egg every day, but Tom could not find the eggs.

The hen's nest was in some high grass. There were twelve eggs in the nest.

One day Tom found the hen sitting on the eggs. He took six of the eggs and gave the hen six duck eggs.

Do you know what happened?

When the eggs were hatched, the hen was very much worried about her babies. She did not know what to do. The little ducks wanted to swim. The chicks did not want to swim. The hen clucked and clucked and clucked. But she could not get the ducks to leave the water.

Jimmy and Alice liked Tom's story. They had a good time at the farm. When they went back to the city they had many things to tell their friends.

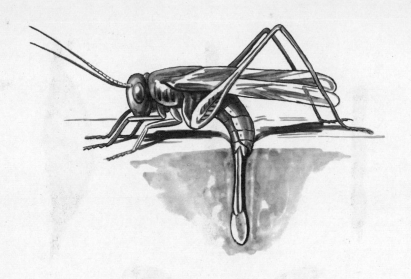

## Insects and Their Eggs

If you look in a grassy field in the spring, you will find some little grasshoppers. The little grasshoppers came from eggs.

The mother grasshopper lays her eggs in the fall. She digs a hole in the hard ground and lays some eggs in it. In the spring the eggs hatch. The little grasshoppers hatch out under the ground. They come above the ground when it is warm.

There are more insects in the world
than any other kind of animals.

All of the pictures on this page show
the same insect. The pictures tell a story.
Can you tell this story?

An insect that does much harm is the clothes moth. This moth lays her eggs in our clothes. The eggs hatch out into little insects that look like worms. The worms eat holes in our clothes. When they grow bigger they make cocoons.

From the cocoons come little moths that have wings. Moths do not eat clothes, but they lay many eggs.

## Alligators

There are big animals that lay eggs, too. Alligators lay their eggs along the banks of streams. Little alligators hatch from the eggs.

Some animals that lay eggs take good care of their babies. Most birds feed their young and protect them. Alligators do not feed their babies or help them in any way.

## How Frogs Grow

Baby robins and all other birds come from eggs. They grow inside the eggs until they are ready to hatch. Then they pick holes in the shells and come out.

The eggs of robins, ducks, and other birds have hard shells. We cannot see through the shells of their eggs.

But frogs lay eggs that have jelly around them. We can see through· the jelly.

Try to get some frogs' eggs and watch them hatch.

Here are some changes that take place
after frogs' eggs hatch.

# The Robin's Nest

One day Alice was looking out of the window. She saw a robin in a tree. The robin sat on a limb and looked about him. He flew to another limb and looked again. Then he flew away.

Soon the robin flew back to the tree. He flew from limb to limb. He looked and looked and looked.

The next day Alice saw two robins in the tree. They brought some straw and other things. They built a nest near the window where Alice could see them.

When the nest was built, the mother robin laid three little blue eggs. She sat on the eggs to keep them warm. Night and day she sat on the eggs. Sometimes the father robin brought her worms to eat. Sometimes she flew away for a time. Then father robin sat on the eggs.

In just two weeks there were three little
robins. How hungry they were! What
big mouths they had! Father and mother
robin were both very busy finding worms
for them to eat.

The young robins ate and ate and grew
and grew. Soon they were almost as large
as their parents. But they did not know
how to fly.

One day there was a big storm. The wind blew hard and broke some of the limbs off the tree. The young robins fell to the ground.

When the storm was over, Alice saw the young robins on the ground. The father and mother robin were worried. They did not know what to do. They could not get their babies back into the nest.

"Jimmy! Come quickly!" cried Alice.

Jimmy came and put the young robins back in the nest. The father and mother robins were very glad.

The next day Alice heard a noise at her window. Here were the father and mother robins. They were trying to tell her that something was wrong. Alice looked and saw a cat in the tree.

"Jimmy! Jimmy!" Alice called again. "The cat is going to eat the robins."

Jimmy came running and pulled the cat out of the tree just in time.

The next day Jimmy's father put a guard on the tree like the one in this picture. Then the cat could not get the robins. Soon they grew strong and flew away.

## Animal Parents

You know that you have two parents. Your parents are your father and your mother.

Your parents find food for you. They give you a place to live. They keep you from harm. There are other things they do for you.

Young animals have two parents just as we do. Most big animals take care of their babies just as your parents take care of you.

Baby woodchucks live in holes in the ground. Their parents take good care of them. Baby frogs live in water. Their parents do not take care of them.

Baby woodchucks look like their parents. But they are not as big as their parents. Baby frogs and baby flies do not look like their parents at all.

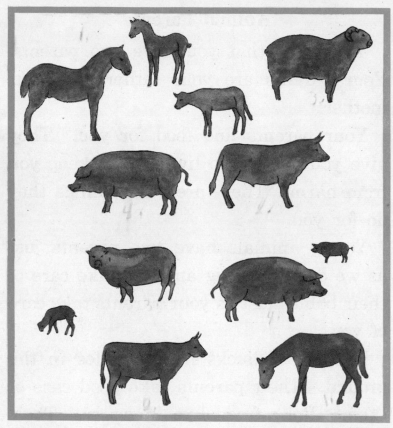

Here are some baby animals and their parents. How many kinds of animals are there?

Can you pick out a father, mother and baby of each kind of animal?

Animals that have hair do not hatch from eggs. They are born alive. Their parents take care of them until they can care for themselves.

Goats are animals that take very good care of their babies.

What does the mother goat do for her babies?

What does the father goat do if you come too near?

Most wild animals take very good care
of their young. Can you tell some things
that wild animals do to protect and care
for their young?

These animals live in other parts of the
world.  Each mother has a different way
of protecting her baby.

How does each animal protect its young?

## Things to Do

1. Gather some cocoons. Try to find different kinds. Watch for the moths to come out of them.

2. Set a hen. Give her plenty of food and clean water. Count the number of days it takes the eggs to hatch.

3. Look for insect eggs under leaves and on branches of trees. Keep the eggs until they hatch.

4. Keep some moths in an insect cage after they come out of the cocoons. They will soon lay eggs.

5. Bring some frogs' eggs to school. Watch the eggs hatch.

6. Find pictures of baby animals and their parents.

7. Visit a farm where you can see young animals and their parents. Find out what the baby animals have to eat.

# Questions

1. Do all animals have parents?

2. Name an animal that hides her babies.

3. Name some animals that hatch from eggs.

4. Name some animals that are born alive.

5. How long does it take a robin's egg to hatch?

6. How do birds care for their babies?

7. How do animals that have hair care for their babies?

8. Name some baby animals that do not look like their parents.

9. Name some baby animals that do look like their parents.

10. Will hens care for little ducks?

11. Where do grasshoppers lay eggs?

12. Name some animals that give milk.

# Do You Know the Right Answers?

1. Most animals have their babies in
   summer    fall    winter    spring
2. Robins' eggs hatch in
   1 week   2 weeks   3 weeks   4 weeks
3. Two animals that lay eggs are
   alligators    flies    goats    cats
4. The number of parents an animal has is
   one    two    three    four
5. Two animals that care for their young are
   alligators           grasshoppers
   goats                woodchucks
6. An animal that sleeps all winter is the
   alligator            grasshopper
   goat                 woodchuck
7. The parents of kids are
   alligators           grasshoppers
   goats                woodchucks

# USEFUL AND HARMFUL
# ANIMALS

## Garden Visitors

When the spring came, Jimmy helped his father plant a garden. First they made the ground ready. Then they planted the seeds.

Soon the baby plants came through the ground. The air got warmer and warmer. The wind blew the clouds across the sky. Rain fell from the clouds, and the baby plants grew bigger and bigger.

Before long, some visitors came to the garden. The visitors were little bugs. Some of the bug visitors ate the leaves of the plants. Others ate the stems. Still others ate the roots. A few of the plants died and some did not grow.

As time went on, bigger animals came
to the garden. Birds came to eat the insects. Toads, snakes, and cats came. All
of the animals were looking for food.

The animals that came to the garden had many babies. The baby animals were always hungry. They kept eating and eating. The more they ate, the bigger they grew. The bigger they grew, the more food they needed.

Some of the insects laid eggs and became the parents of other insects. But many of them were eaten by other animals.

The robins and some other birds had their nests near the garden. The young robins opened their mouths for worms. The father and mother robins were always busy finding worms to feed their babies.

Snakes, toads and other animals were busy catching the insects. But cats came to catch the birds, snakes, and toads. The cats' babies were hungry, too.

All summer there was a race to see whose babies would be fed. Animals ate many of the plants. Animals ate each other. But there were some plants for Jimmy and Alice to eat.

Some of the insects were alive at the end of the summer. Some of the little toads grew into big toads. Some of the snakes grew into bigger snakes. The young robins grew larger and flew away. And the kittens grew into cats.

## Useful Garden Animals

Some of the animals that live in the garden are very helpful. We should not harm them.

Here are a few of the garden animals that help us. They help us by eating other animals. Try to find out more about them.

The most useful animals in the garden are the birds. A bird will eat hundreds and hundreds of insects every day.

If there were no birds, there would be more insects every year. Soon there would be so many insects that they would eat all the green plants. Then there would be no food for the other animals.

Do you know the bird in the picture? What other birds do you know? What can we do to protect the birds?

## Animals That Give Us Food
## and Clothes

Another animal that is very useful is the cow. Here are some of the things that we get from cows. Can you name others?

In some parts of the world there are no cows. It is too hot or too cold for them to live in some places. In other places it is too dry and there is not enough food.

Where there are no cows, the people get milk from other animals. Each animal in the picture on this page is used for milk in some part of the world.

The meat of these animals is also used for food. The hair or wool of some of them is used for making clothes.

Another way that animals help us is by doing work. Can you name some kinds of work that horses do?

Animals that work hard all day need plenty of good food. They get thirsty and need clean water to drink. At night they need a good place to sleep.

Do you think the animal in this picture has good care? How can you tell?

In all parts of the world, animals work for men.

Dogs are used in the far North. Their warm coats protect them from the cold.

The camel is used where it is very dry. A camel can live for days without a drink. It can store much water in its body.

Elephants can lift heavy weights. They can work where it is very hot.

Water buffaloes are used where the land is wet. They have big, flat feet.

The animals in this picture are both harmful and useful.

Can you name other animals that are both harmful and useful?

## Animals We Like to Watch

People who live in the country see many animals. Animals live in the woods and other places. It is fun to watch the animals.

People who live in the city like to watch animals, too. In every big city there is a zoo. Animals are brought to the zoo from places far away.

Did you ever go to a zoo? Where is the nearest zoo? What animals in the zoo do you like most?

Which of these animals would you like
for a pet? Do you have a good place to
keep this pet? Could you get the right
food for it? Tell what else you would
have to do to give this pet good care.

Do you know any other animals that
are kept for pets?

# Tell the Right Answer

1. Animals that eat the most insects are
   cows    birds    sheep    cats

2. An animal that gives milk is the
   frog    robin    fly    goat

3. An animal that does work is the
   chicken    toad    camel    snake

4. An animal that gives us meat is the
   cat    lion    sheep    toad

5. An animal that eats other animals is the
   frog    cow    horse    camel

6. An animal that gives us wool is the
   horse    pig    sheep    frog

7. An animal that can store much water in its body is the
   cow    horse    camel    sheep

8. An animal that makes a good pet is the
   frog    toad    lion    dog

# Questions

1. Why did so many animals come to the garden?

2. Name a useful insect.

3. Name a harmful insect.

4. What would happen if there were no birds?

5. What are some other animals that we should protect?

6. What three animals do you think are most useful? Why do you think so?

7. Name some animals that do work.

8. Name some things you use that come from animals.

9. Name some animals that give milk.

10. In what different ways are sheep useful?

11. Name an animal that is both harmful and useful.

12. What animals make the best pets?

## How Much Do You Remember?

1. What kinds of foods do animals eat?

2. Where do animals get their food?

3. How are animals protected?

4. How do animals prepare for winter?

5. How do animals live in winter?

6. How do people prepare for winter?

7. In what forms is water found?

8. How may water change its form?

9. How does water get into the air?

10. What do magnets do?

11. How are magnets used?

12. What shape is the earth?

13. Why do things stay on the earth?

14. Do all animals have parents?

15. How do animals care for their young?

16. How are animals helpful and harmful?

17. How should we care for our pets?

## What kinds of leaves are these?

## What animal babies are these?

## What foods do these animals eat?

1

2

3

4

What will happen next?

1

2

3

4

What will happen next?

1

2

3

4

What will happen next?

What are these plants and animals?

7  8  12  9  11  10

Where have you seen them before?

## Which animal hatched from an egg?

## Which animal is not an insect?

## Which animal was born alive?

Are these animals useful or harmful?

From what animals do we get these foods?

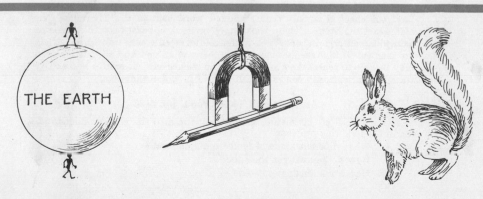

What is wrong in each of these pictures?

# NOTES

The world of science and nature is a new world of adventure for children. Wonder, or child curiosity, given encouragement and direction, leads to all the thrills that accompany real learning of the truths of science. The authors believe that truth is fascinating and properly emotional in its appeal to young adventurers in science. These books are written in the language of children and with the most careful regard for accuracy of content. The authors believe also that learning in science should be an integral part of an elementary school program which is designed to help children live happily in their social and physical worlds. The material included in these science books was carefully planned with respect to childhood interests and needs and arranged in accordance with the seasons so as to promote real learning through the use of a wealth of available materials and appropriate activities.

The activities and exercises described and suggested are arranged in a natural learning sequence as determined by careful trial in a large number of typical urban and rural elementary school classrooms. The science materials are organized in a flexible learning-unit form which facilitates adaptation to local programs of study and permits their use as the motivating cores or important parts of larger projects in an integrated elementary school curriculum. The content was carefully checked with curriculum materials proposed in various State Syllabuses and in such reports as the 31st Yearbook of the National Society for the Study of Education. The rich and comprehensive content represents the contribution of research in elementary school science and of a long experience with a nature study program in American elementary schools.

In the construction of these books, major attention has been given to the reading problem. Child language and simplicity of vocabulary dominate the style of the reading material. The illustrations were carefully planned along with the text and present a most worthwhile series of science learning experiences. The manuscript was carefully checked by experienced classroom teachers and by reading experts, line by line and page by page. The vocabulary was checked against such standard word lists as the Thorndike, the Gates and the Stone. These books may be used as basal texts in science or as reading material in connection with an integrated course in reading. They are planned so that reading may be a means to an end and so that children may be able to center their interests in the science subject matter and satisfy their natural curiosity concerning the world in which they live.

## Animals and Their Food, pp. 5-36

The materials of this section should contribute to the child's understanding of the following problems:

A. What different kinds of food do animals eat?
B. How do animals get their food?
C. How are animals protected?

A field trip with the purpose of observing animals getting food will serve as an excellent approach.

Page 6. Great blue heron, beaver swimming.

7. Red-tailed hawk, gray squirrel, snapping turtle. A study of this illustration will show how these animals are fitted for food getting and protection.

8. Grass furnishes more food for animals than any other material.

10. Grasshoppers may be kept in the schoolroom in a covered glass jar or aquarium. Cover the bottom with sod and keep it moist.

11. June bug on wild rose. There are more insects in the world than any other kind of animal

12. Oak, maple, sassafras, and elm leaves. Notice the missing portions.

13. Children should now be able to use the term "insects" correctly. Harebells in border.

14. Another interesting way to catch insects is to hold an inverted umbrella under a bush and shake the bush.

15. Bumblebee on delphinium.

17–18. The fact that a frog's tongue is sticky also aids in catching insects.

20. (1) Many kinds of animals have no teeth. (2) Children will be interested in counting their own teeth. (3) The front teeth are used for cutting and the back teeth for grinding foods. (4) No modern bird has teeth.

21. Tracks of a duck and the forefoot of a dog, a rabbit, and a cat are shown in this order.

26. Bald eagle, downy woodpecker, pelican.

27. Barn swallow catching May fly.

29. Blacksnake. Snakes do not chew their food.

32. (1) Cow. (2) Bird. (3) Cat. (4) Flowers. (5) Leaves. (6) Animals. (7) Grass. (8) Plants. (9) Grasshopper.

34. Horned toad, praying mantis.

35. Bear, porcupine, painted turtle, skunk.

36. Sample answers to first list: (1) Seeds. (2) Grass. (3) Nectar. (4) Bananas. (5) Grass. (6) Lettuce. (7) Grass.

Sample answers to second list: (1) Grasshoppers. (2) Rabbits. (3) Beavers. (4) Fruit flies. (5) Insects. (6) Bees.

## Getting Ready for Winter, pp. 37-60

Problems:

 *A.* How do animals prepare for winter?

 *B.* How do animals live in winter?

 *C.* How do people prepare for winter?

38–39. A study of the illustration will reveal many signs of winter. A field trip or observation from the window will reveal others.

40. The cheeks of chipmunks are fur-lined pouches. The chipmunk shown has gathered more nuts than he can carry.

42. The moths shown are Cecropia, Promethea, and Luna.

43–44. Watch for migrating birds. Most bird migration is a result of a reduced food supply and not cold weather.

45. Alligators and flamingo in a Florida cypress swamp.

46. Prickly pear, jack-rabbit, and armadillo (Texas).

48. Cross section of woodchuck burrow. Rabbits and other animals sometimes use the empty rooms while the woodchuck is asleep.

49. Bat, bear, raccoon, jumping mouse.

50. Red ant carrying aphid into burrow.

51–52. The winter food supply of beavers consists of sections of trees which are sunk to the bottom of ponds and fastened down. After the bark is eaten from them, the wood is used for building houses and dams.

57. Children will enjoy carrying on this activity themselves.

59. Various possible answers to these questions are found in the text.

60. (1) No. (2) Yes. (3) No. (4) Yes. (5) Yes. (6) Yes. (7) No. (8) Yes. (9) Yes. (10) Yes. (11) No. (12) No. (13) No. (14) Yes.

## Water and Its Forms, pp. 61-80

Problems:

A. In what forms is water found?

B. How may water change its form?

C. How does water get into the air?

D. How do living things use water?

62–63. Young children have difficulty in distinguishing facts from fancies. Here is an opportunity to develop the distinction.

65. Snow, ice, rain, clouds, and steam are all forms of water.

66–67. The activities listed on page 66 should provide a basis for answering the questions on page 67. The following answers are considered satisfactory at this age level:

(1) When water is cooled sufficiently it changes into ice. (2) Adding heat. (3) Adding heat. (4) Yes. (5) Yes, by sufficient cooling. (6) Snow is frozen water vapor. (7) No. (8) It changes into water or ice. (9) Yes. (10) No. (11) Yes. (12) Yes. (13) Snow, ice, hail, dew, steam, water vapor. (14) Ice, snow, hail, sleet, frost.

68. The water cycle will be a new concept for most children. A careful study of the illustration should make it clear.

71. It is usually advisable to avoid the term "evaporate" at this level.

73. The water from the jar kept in a hot place will pass into the air most rapidly, and from the jar in the cold place least rapidly.

75. Niagara Falls.

76. Above: leopard shark, lobster; below: octopus, squid.

77. Reindeer and timber wolf.

79. Answers to questions will vary but all questions are answered in text.

80. (1) Steam. (2) Wind. (3) Heat. (4) Water. (5) Ice. (6) Vapor. (7) Clouds. (8) Skin. (9) Mouth.

## Magnets, pp. 81-92

Problems:

    *A.* What do magnets do?

    *B.* How are magnets used?

Magnets of various shapes and sizes, lodestones, corks, pieces of iron and steel, steel knitting needles and other materials should be available during the study of this section.

84. Children have many superstitions based upon no more concrete evidence than was the belief in sea monsters.

85. The little balls shown in the illustration are those commonly used in air rifles. They are available everywhere.

86. Fish for this game can easily be made by running steel pins through small pieces of wood.

87. Magnets should work through paper, wood and glass.

88. Every magnet, no matter how small, has two poles where the magnetic attraction is greatest.

90. Making a compass is really very easy. All that is necessary is to suspend a magnet in some way that will allow it to turn freely.

92. First list: (1) A magnet will attract anything made of iron or steel. (2) The needle of a compass will point north and south. (3) Many magnet games are common in addition to the one mentioned in the text. (4) Rubbing a piece of steel over a magnet will magnetize the steel. (5) A compass can be made by suspending a small magnet so that it turns freely.

Second list: (1) Yes. (2) No. (3) No. (4) No. (5) No. (6) Yes. (7) No.

## The Earth, pp. 93-108

Problems:

    *A.* What shape is the earth?

    *B.* Why do things stay on the earth?

    *C.* What is there around the earth?

94–95. This sketch was made in New York harbor.

97. The earth is really spherical but, in child language, it is round.

99. Scene in New Guinea: natives, huts and coconut palms.

100. The dolls are from Japan, Alaska, Australia and South America.

102. The same dolls are shown in proper position on the globe.

105. This is another opportunity to bring out the differences between science and unfounded beliefs.

107. Answers to questions: (1–2) Gravity. (3) The earth is very big. (4) Gravity. (5) The curvature of the earth can be observed directly from a high place looking out over the ocean. (6) It takes a long time for ships to go around the earth. (7) Air. (8) Nothing would stay on the earth. (9) Away from the center of the earth. (10) Toward the center of the earth. (11) The weight of any object is due to the pull of gravity. (12) Gravity.

## Animals and Their Babies, pp. 109-134

Problems:

    *A.*  Do all animals have parents?

    *B.*  What animals come from eggs?

    *C.*  How do animals care for their young?

One of the best projects to accompany the work of this section is to secure a hen that is ready to set and have her carry on the incubation in the schoolroom. Appoint children to give her food and water and cultivate an attitude of protection on their part.

118.  Cecropia moth: egg, larva, pupa, and adult.

119.  Development of clothes moth. Only the larva eats clothes.

121.  Mass of frogs' eggs in battery jar. Eggs hatching at right.

122.  Stages in the development of the bullfrog: egg, shortly after hatching, young tadpole, year-old tadpole, appearance of hind legs, appearance of front legs, nearly adult.

123–126.  This is a true story and is told exactly as it happened.

133.  Answers will vary. Questions based on text and illustrations.

134.  (1) Spring. (2) Two weeks. (3) Alligators and flies. (4) Two. (5) Goats and woodchucks. (6) Woodchuck. (7) Goats.

## Useful and Harmful Animals, pp. 135-152

Problems:

    *A.*  In what different ways do animals help us?

    *B.*  In what different ways are animals harmful?

    *C.*  How should we select and care for our pets?

Make a collection and study of animal products. Try to discover the source of as many as possible; for example, frankfurters, suet, steak, etc.

138.  Wire worm on cabbage root, potato beetle on potato plant.

139.  Cabbage worm on tomato plant, bluebird, garter snake, toad.

142.  The mantis, dragonfly and ladybird beetle all eat harmful insects.

143.  Song sparrow.

145.  Dromedary, llama, yak.

147.  Top: dog sled and huskies; bottom: water buffalo.

148.  Starling, raccoon, ground mole.

149.  Dog-faced baboon.

150.  Parrot, canary, monkey, goldfish, terrier, guinea pig, rabbit, cat, duck.

151.  (1) Birds. (2) Goat. (3) Camel. (4) Sheep. (5) Frog. (6) Sheep. (7) Camel. (8) Dog.

## How Much Do You Remember? pp. 153-159

The purpose of these test materials is to suggest methods of evaluating the science understandings of pupils rather than to provide a set final examination. Tests of these types are most valuable when they are teacher-constructed and are used systematically throughout the year for the purpose of measuring pupil progress.

153. These questions are answered on the following pages: (1) pp. 7–11; (2) pp. 16–19, 24–30; (3) pp. 31, 34–35; (4) pp. 40–44; (5) pp. 45–54; (6) pp. 55–56; (7) pp. 64–66; (8) pp. 66–75; (9) pp. 73–74; (10) pp. 85–88; (11) pp. 88–90; (12) p. 97; (13) pp. 101–104; (14) pp. 111–119; (15) 123–131; (16) pp. 137–148; (17) p. 150.

154. Top: oak, maple, sassafras. Middle: lamb, skunk, pig. Bottom: the beaver eats the bark of trees; the fox eats rabbits, mice and other animals; the squirrel eats nuts.

155. Top: front legs appear, hind legs grow larger and tail becomes smaller. Middle: the moth comes out of the cocoon. Bottom: the young robins are fed.

156. (1) Cactus, (2) swallow, (3) delphinium, (4) water lily, (5) pelican, (6) turtle.

157. (7) Bat, (8) geranium, (9) horned toad, (10) skunk, (11) trout, (12) wild rose.

158. Top: alligator. Middle: snake. Bottom: rabbit.

159. Top: all are useful. Middle: bee, hen, cow. Bottom: the feet of both figures should be against the earth; a magnet does not attract a pencil; the rabbit has a squirrel's tail.

# WORD LIST

The following list contains all the new words—337 in number—used in this book, aside from those already used in Book I of this series. Approximately 90 per cent of the words used in Book II are found in the Gates: A READING VOCABULARY FOR THE ELEMENTARY GRADES (Revised and Enlarged). Out of the 337 words, 126 are in the First 500, 103 in the Second 500, 56 in the Third 500, and 16 in the Fourth 500 of the Gates list. The remaining 36 words are either proper names or are explained in the context.

**7**
busy

**8**
wonder
watch
first
field
ate

**9**
wild
into
deer
ran
bushes

**10**
let's
grasshopper
jump
began

**11**
children
farther
pulled
insects
legs

**13**
piece
flies
jar
different
been

**14**
catch
eyes
mouth

**15**
game
sometimes
visit
each

**16**
sweet
bees
tongue
draws
roll

**17**
frog
funny
happened
fast
caught
never

**18**
fastened
front
his

**19**
teeth
sharp
flat
horses
sheep

**20**
answer
question
cat's

**21**
tracks
foot
stamp
pad
dog
rabbit

**23**
circus
which
drink
seen

**24**
hawks
mouse
noses
ears
smell
might

**25**
her
closely
soft
claws

**26**
bills
wings

**27**
worms
snake

**28**
by
lying
even
seem
often

**29**
just
inside
lump
body
don't

**30**
another
mosquitoes

**31**
protect
themselves
hard
stay
enough

**32**
butterflies

**33**
both

**34**
enemies

**37**
ready

**39**
morning
blew
falling
coat
feels

**40**
gone
brown
nuts
guess

**41**
die
summer
store
lay
cocoons

**43**
heard
noise
cried

**44**
blackbirds

**46**
country
dry
easily
plenty

**47**
woodchuck
walking
hole
listen
hear

**48**
asleep
yet
fat

**49**
breath
slowly

**50**
nests
ants
take
honey
rats
mice

**51**
beavers
cut
bark

**52**
building
door

**53**
fox
chickens

**54**
mud

**55**
people

**56**
cool
easy
wear
clothes
should

**57**
story
wore
same

**58**
stand
together
shade

**59**
heavy

**61**
forms

**63**
true
else

**64**
real
reason

**65**
again

**66**
steam
outside
freeze
salt
mark

**68**
alive
drop
stop

**69**
melts
waves

**70**
pan
mine

**71**
next
full
maybe
drank
laughed
tomorrow

**72**
sill
whether
wash
blackboard

**73**
learned

**74**
called
vapor
ponds

**75**
river
ocean
page
shows
waterfall
fell

**77**
toads
thirsty
puddle
skin

**78**
shown

**80**
iron
caused
feet

**81**
magnets

**82**
ships
ago
afraid
sail
lost

**84**
years
compass
needle
across

**86**
pole

**87**
tell
tie
string
touch

**88**
lift
pick

**89**
rub
steel
direction

**91**
turn

**95**
grandfather
trip
dock
mother

**96**
last
rise

**97**
over
remember
yesterday

**98**
glad
who

**99**
side

**100**
brought
presents
best
dolls

**101**
globe
blue
tape
upside
off

**103**
nothing
toward
gravity

**104**
center
strange
book
weigh
yourself
stick

**105**
thought
elephant
turtle

**106**
thick
empty
space

**107**
throw

**108**
leave

**109**
babies

**111**
Easter
cousins
Tom
Betty
took

**112**
petted
hurt

**113**
hungry
care
young

**114**
dried
hair

**115**
laid
egg
twelve
hen
sitting

**116**
hatched
worried
chicks
clucked
friends

**119**
moth
wing

**120**
alligator
banks
feed

**121**
shells
jelly
robins

**123**
robin's
limb
flew
straw
built
three

**124**
weeks
grew
almost
parents

**125**
storm
broke
quickly

**126**
wrong
guard

**127**
harm

**129**
born
goats

**132**
gather
set
clean
number
branches
cage

**134**
kids

**137**
visitors

**138**
bugs

**141**
race
fed
end
kittens

**143**
hundreds

**145**
meat
wool

**146**
work

**147**
men
camel
buffaloes
wet

**149**
zoo
most

**150**
kept

**151**
lion